# Where Is the International Space Station?

by Dana Meachen Rau

illustrated by Dede Putra

Penguin Workshop

To all those who dream big and make it happen
—DMR

PENGUIN WORKSHOP
An imprint of Penguin Random House LLC
1745 Broadway, New York, NY 10019
penguinrandomhouse.com

Library of Congress Cataloging-in-Publication Data is available.

First published in the United States of America by Penguin Workshop, 2026

Manufactured in the United States of America
CJKW

ISBN 9798217051342 (paperback)
10 9 8 7 6 5 4 3 2 1

ISBN 9798217051359 (library binding)
10 9 8 7 6 5 4 3 2 1

The authorized representative in the EU for product safety and compliance is Penguin Random House Ireland, Morrison Chambers, 32 Nassau Street, Dublin D02 YH68, Ireland, https://eu-contact.penguin.ie.

## Contents

Zarya module

# Where Is the International Space Station?

On December 6, 1998, a construction crew began working on a huge building project. But it wasn't a usual construction site with bulldozers, dump trucks, traffic cones, or workers in hard hats. This crew was made up of astronauts. They were putting together pieces of the International Space Station (ISS), and they were doing it about 250 miles above Earth!

A Russian spacecraft had delivered the first piece, called Zarya, into Earth's orbit on November 20, 1998. This module had been waiting more than two weeks for the United States' space shuttle *Endeavour* to arrive with another module called Unity.

*Endeavour* opened the doors of its large payload

bay (an area that holds the cargo of the spaceship). Unity was carefully nestled inside with little room to spare. Docking two huge modules together in space would not be a simple job. And they were all traveling 17,500 miles per hour. That's five miles per second!

Shuttle astronaut Nancy Currie controlled the shuttle's robotic arm. She was nervous, even though she had been training for two and a half years for this moment. She sat at the controls. Her view out the window was blocked, so Nancy had to rely on monitors to line up the modules. Very carefully, she moved the arm to reach out and grab Zarya. She pulled the module closer to Unity, where it was still connected to the shuttle's payload bay. She also used some of the thrusters on *Endeavour* to better

Nancy Currie

line the pieces up. Even though the modules were designed to fit together, they had been built in different countries by different teams. Everyone hoped they would connect as planned.

All of Currie's training paid off! The two pieces locked together. She could finally breathe again. The first step in the construction of the International Space Station was a success!

Piece by piece, modules and other parts would be brought up and assembled in orbit. Within a

few years, crews would be living and working on the ISS. By 2011, with the help of fifteen nations, construction was finally complete. After that, even more pieces were added.

Since it was first occupied more than twenty years ago, the ISS has been a scientific laboratory orbiting around Earth. Inside its many modules, crews of astronauts perform experiments. These astronauts have come from the United States, Russia, and many other countries. They have made amazing discoveries about space, our planet, and even the human body. The hard work done on the ISS benefits everyone on Earth.

Discoveries from the International Space Station will help us in the future, too. Scientists and engineers plan to travel beyond our orbit. All we have learned from the ISS has prepared them to venture to other planets and deeper into space to discover even more about the universe we call home.

# CHAPTER 1
# Science and Imagination

Life on Earth thousands of years ago was very different from today. People spent their days gathering and hunting for food. They found or built shelters to protect them from fierce animals and harsh weather. They lived in groups to keep one another safe.

In the evenings, they looked into the sky and were curious about what they saw. They didn't know then that the thousands of tiny lights were stars and planets. They didn't know that the moon seemed to change shape because the sun's light reflected off of it as it circled around Earth. They didn't have the science or technology to learn more about objects in the sky.

Over time, people noticed patterns and developed ideas about what they saw. Ancient Greeks, about 2,500 years ago, were the first to suggest that Earth was round. They observed how a round shadow fell across the moon during an eclipse. (That's because the shadow is from Earth.) They watched the way stars seemed to move together in the same direction, while other bright dots seemed to wander. (The stars seemed to move because Earth was turning, and the dots wandered because they were planets moving on their own paths.) They also noticed that just the top of a ship could be seen from a distance. (That's because the horizon was not flat.) All these things suggested that Earth was round.

Ptolemy

The Egyptian astronomer Ptolemy, who lived in the second century CE, believed

that Earth was the center of space. He suggested that the stars, moon, planets, and sun each moved around Earth in their own circle-shaped paths. People believed this idea for a long time.

Then in the 1500s, Polish astronomer Nicolaus Copernicus suggested that the sun was at the center. The invention of the telescope in the 1600s led to the discovery of even more planets orbiting the sun. This gave us the model of the solar system as we know it today.

Nicolaus Copernicus

Today, we know that the sun is a large star at the center of our solar system. It has a lot of gravity. Gravity is the pull of one object on another. The sun's gravity is strong enough to pull on eight large bodies of rock and gas—the planets. These planets travel around the sun in their own regular paths, called orbits. Each planet's orbit is unique—some planets take a very long time to complete an orbit around the sun, and others do so very quickly. Mercury takes only eighty-eight days to orbit the sun. Meanwhile, it takes Neptune 60,190 days to complete its orbit. Earth takes 365 days, which is why we have 365 days in one year.

All the planets, including Earth, also have gravity. Without Earth's gravity, people and objects would be weightless—which means they would

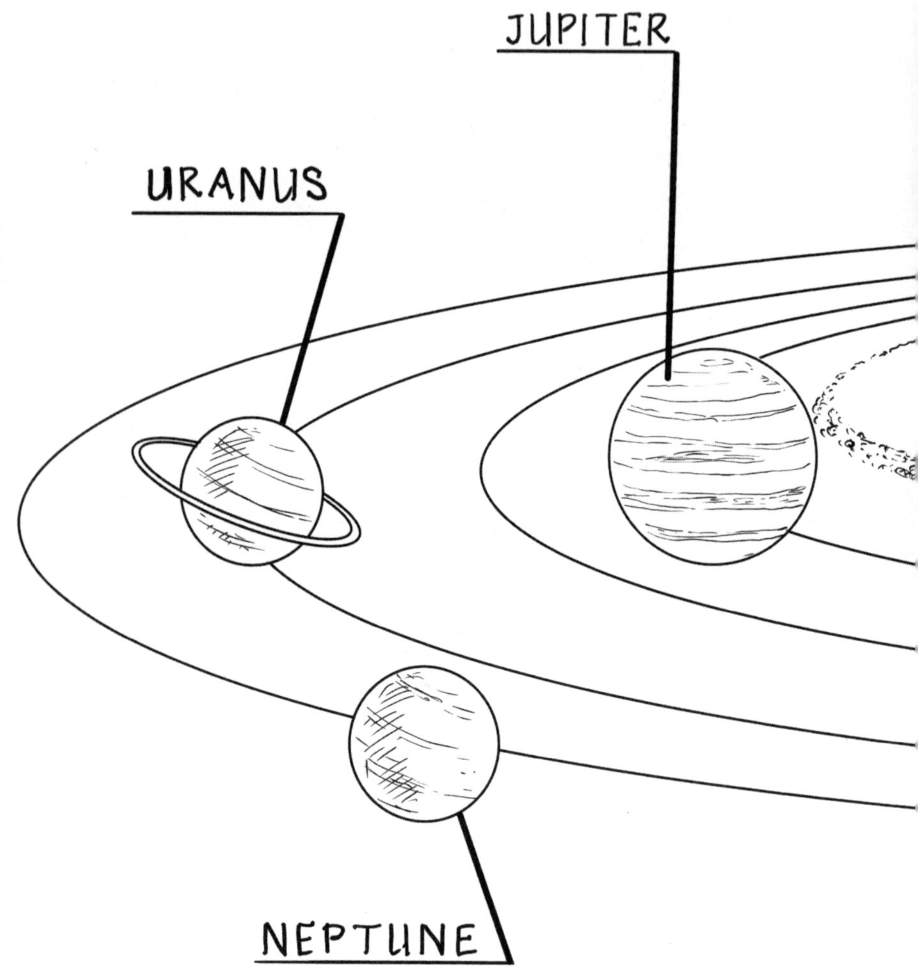

float off into space. Earth's gravity also pulls on large objects in space, like the moon. This gravity keeps the moon in Earth's orbit.

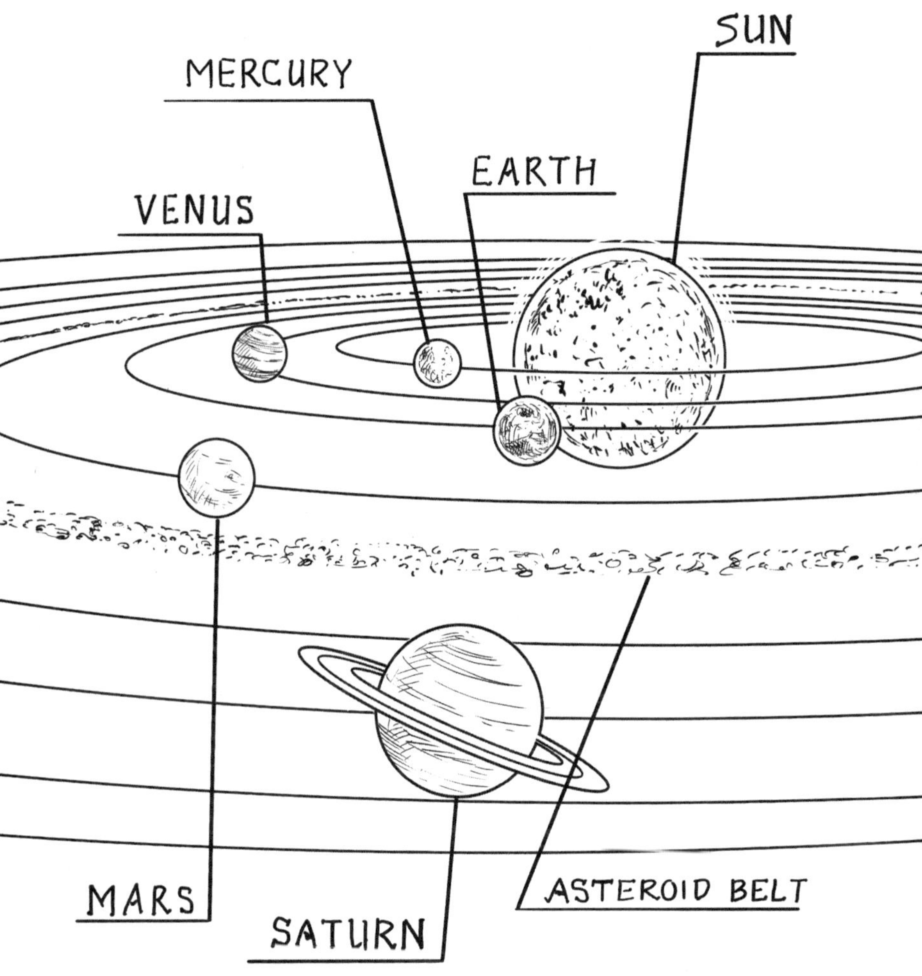

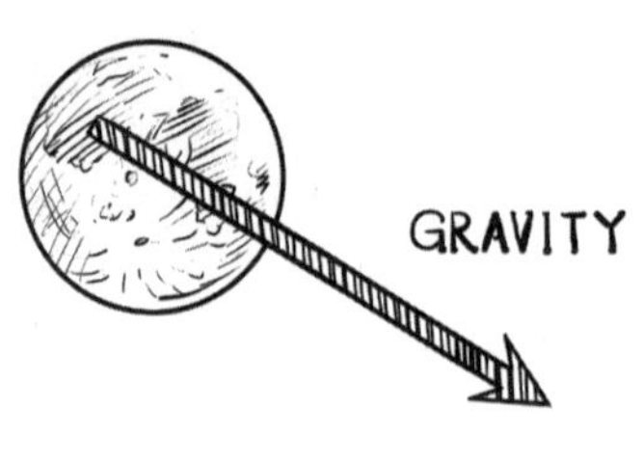


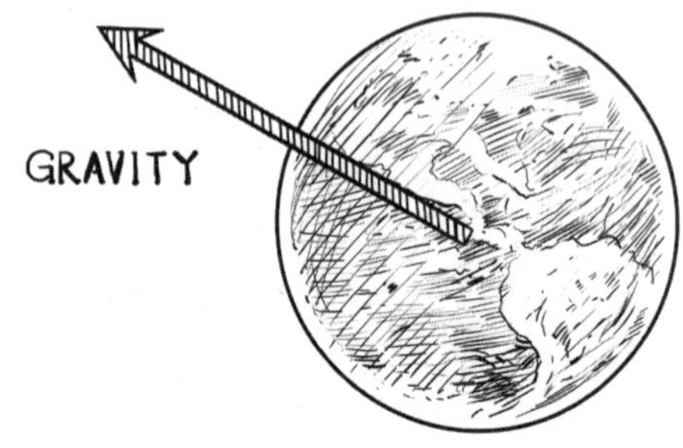


As people discovered how space worked, they asked themselves, *What if?* What if we could travel to the moon or the planets? What if people could live in space?

Writers used their imaginations to make up stories about space travel. Jules Verne's book *From the Earth to the Moon*, published in 1865, imagined that a giant cannon could shoot a spacecraft to the moon. In 1869, Edward Everett Hale wrote a short story called "The Brick Moon." People consider this the first story to imagine what a space station might look like. In the story, the space station is a two-hundred-foot hollow sphere made of brick. It launches by rolling down a hill, and then two wheels fling it into the sky. The people back on Earth watch the space travelers living and working on the brick moon's surface through their telescopes.

Imagining space travel wasn't just for writers. Scientists thought about space stations, too. In 1928, Herman "Noordung" Potočnik designed a wheel-shaped station that looked like a giant donut. It would rotate, or spin, to create gravity for the crew as they performed experiments and observed Earth. Wernher von Braun, a rocketry scientist, developed his own station idea. His station was also wheel shaped and would be able to hold eighty people at a time.

Stories and movies continued to imagine what

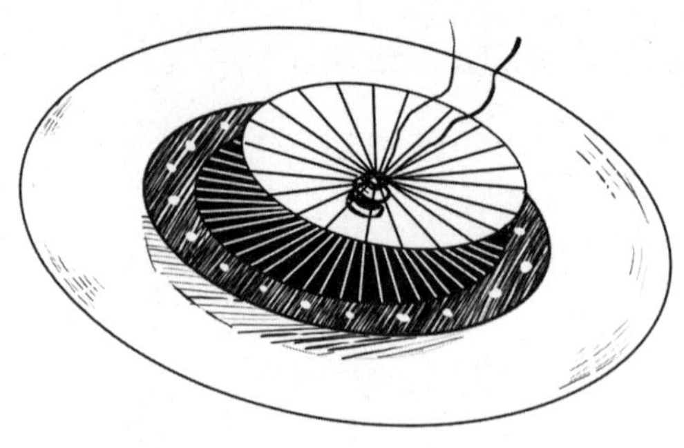

Noordung's imagined space station

living in space would be like. But that wasn't real life—it was fiction. The more scientists learned about the environment beyond Earth's atmosphere, the more they discovered it would be very difficult to live anywhere besides our own planet.

On Earth, the atmosphere, which is made up of the gases around our planet, protects us from the harshness of space. The atmosphere provides oxygen, which is the chemical element that humans need to breathe in order to survive. Our atmosphere also keeps temperatures from getting too hot or too cold. It protects us from the

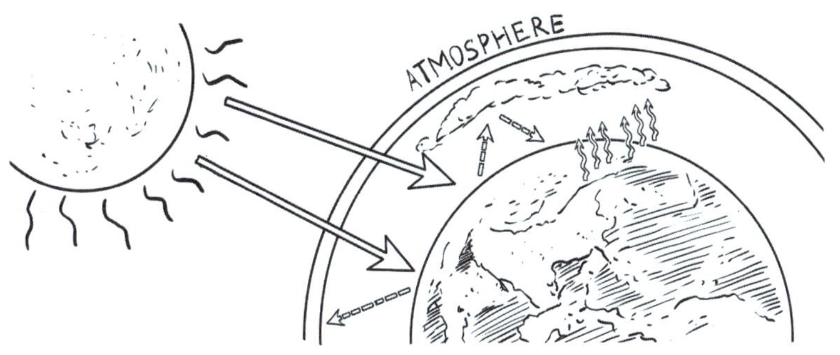


harmful rays of the sun. Its air pressure keeps the fluids in our body working as they should. But in space, there is no protection.

Scientists still couldn't help asking, *What if?* What if they could somehow create safe ways for people to travel in space? Both science and imagination would be needed to complete this big goal.

## The Nebra Sky Disc

The Nebra Sky Disc is thought to be the oldest map of space. It is a flat circle, only about twelve inches across, that is made up of copper, bronze, and gold.

Treasure hunters claim to have dug it up on a hill called Mittelberg near the present-day village of Nebra in Germany in 1999. It was missing for a few years until it was recovered by the police and other authorities in 2002.

The disc shows a bunch of gold stars. A crescent shape represents the moon, and the round shape is believed to be either the sun or a full moon. But not all archaeologists (people whose job it is to study items left behind by past cultures) agree on the other images. Some think the arches on each side are horizons. They think that the arch on the bottom is a boat. Others think the arch may be a rainbow.

Archaeologists also don't agree on the disc's age or where it was found. If the treasure hunters' story is true, the disc would be 3,600 years old. If not, it may be one thousand years younger. If that's the case, then it isn't the oldest image of the sky.

Either way, the disc is an interesting look at how ancient people thought about space.

## CHAPTER 2
## Racing to Space

During the mid-1900s, scientists developed rockets that were large, powerful, and fast enough to travel beyond Earth's atmosphere. Starting in the 1950s, two countries—the United States and the Soviet Union—both wanted to be the leader in space exploration. They competed to achieve important "firsts" in space. This competition became known as the space race.

The Daily

SATELLITE FIRED BY RUSSIA;
CIRCLING US 15 TIMES A DAY

The space race began on October 4, 1957, when the Soviet Union launched Sputnik 1. *Sputnik* is the Russian word for "fellow traveler." Sputnik was a sphere of metal, about the size of a beach ball. It was the first artificial satellite to orbit Earth. Sputnik was uncrewed, which means there were no people on board.

Sputnik 1

## Artificial Satellites

A satellite is an object that orbits around another larger object. Earth has a large natural satellite—the moon. But thousands of artificial, or human-made, satellites orbit Earth, too.

Scientists and companies send these satellites into space for many reasons. Some satellites help people communicate by sending phone, television, or internet signals. GPS satellites control systems that help us navigate from place to place. Others are used to monitor the atmosphere so that humans can predict the weather. Many satellites collect information about Earth and space for scientists.

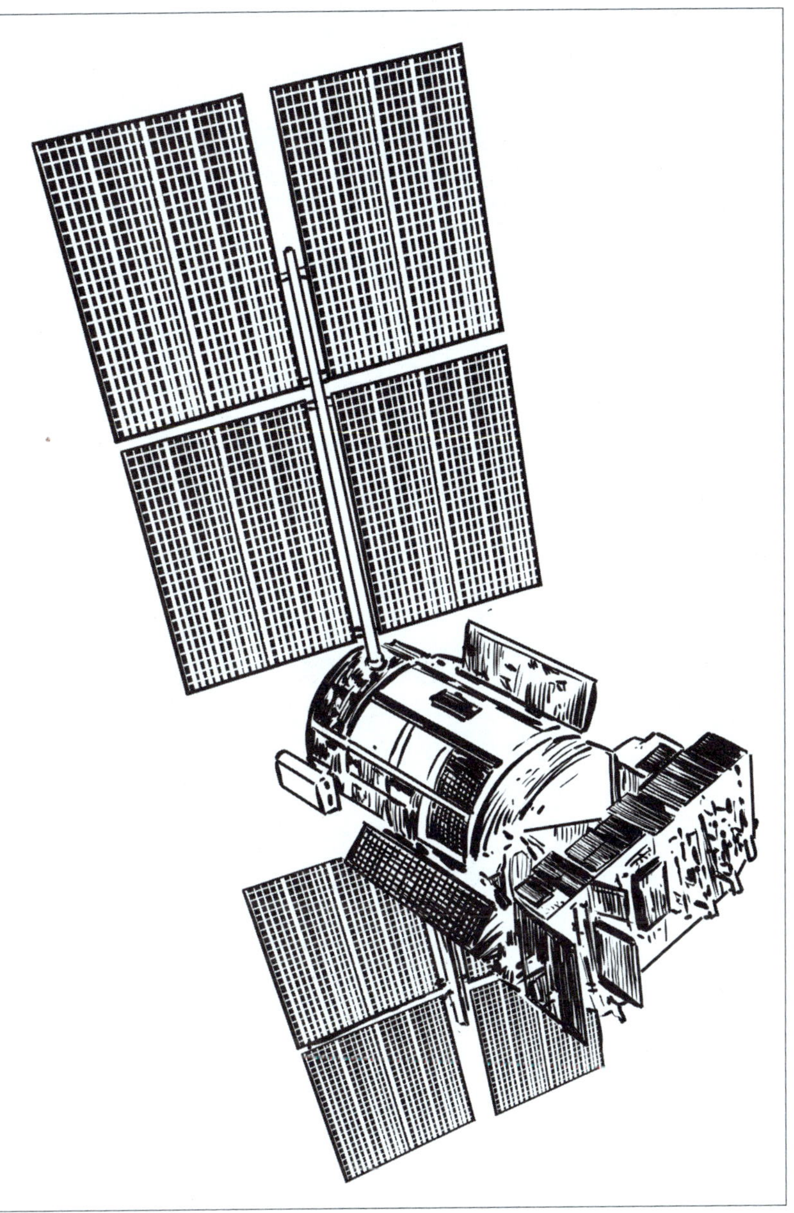

Yuri Gagarin

Next, the Soviets and Americans raced to be the first to send a crewed spacecraft into orbit. The Soviets won that "first," too. On April 12, 1961, pilot Yuri Gagarin orbited once around Earth and became the first person in space. A little less than a month later, American pilot Alan Shepard became the second.

The United States was losing the space race. In 1961, President John F. Kennedy announced that America would reach the moon within ten years. The National Aeronautics and Space Administration (NASA) went to work. In July 1969, NASA sent the Apollo 11 mission to the moon, and two astronauts walked on its surface for the first time.

Now that humans had been in space, both nations focused on designing and building space stations. These spacecraft would serve as orbiting

space laboratories. Astronauts would live and work on them for long periods of time.

The Soviets built the first successful space station. On April 19, 1971, they launched Salyut 1. Over the next ten years, they sent six more Salyuts into orbit as well. In 1986, the Soviets launched Mir. This space station was made up of sections (called modules) that were assembled in space.

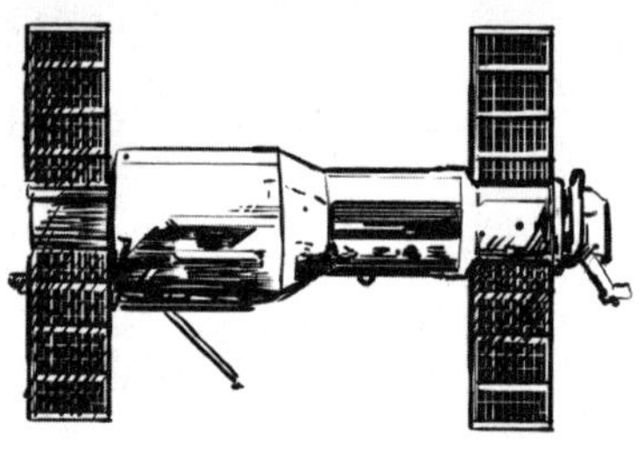

Salyut 1

Meanwhile, NASA used equipment left over from their Apollo missions to build Skylab, which launched in 1973. Three astronauts lived there at a time. They observed our planet and space from a new view. They also studied how the weightless environment inside the station affected their bodies and other materials. Skylab was meant to be temporary. It lasted less than a year. The United States then turned its focus, time, money, and technology to the Space Shuttle program instead.

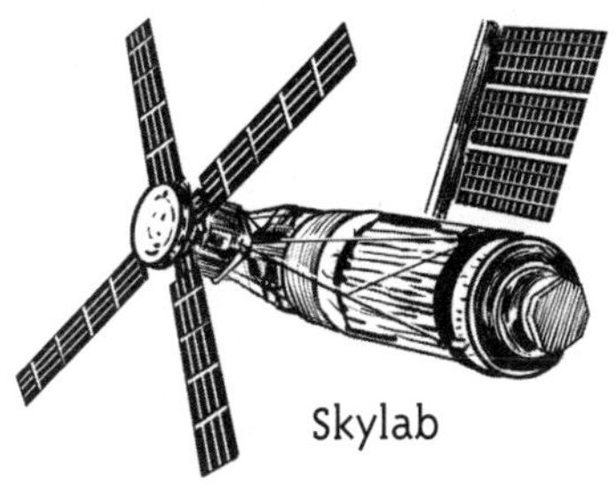
Skylab

Up to this point, rockets had launched, delivered spacecraft into orbit, and fallen back to Earth through the atmosphere, where they would burn up. Astronauts would return to Earth by locking themselves into capsules that could withstand Earth's atmosphere. These capsules would fall into the ocean and be rescued by a team back on Earth. Spacecraft cost a lot to build, so burning them up began to seem like a waste of money and equipment as more and more missions were sent into space.

Space shuttles, on the other hand, were reusable. Rocket boosters and a giant fuel tank helped launch the shuttle's orbiter into space. The rockets fell off, landed in the ocean, and were used again. The orbiter orbited around Earth. When it was time to come home, it could safely reenter the atmosphere and land similar to the way a plane lands on a runway.

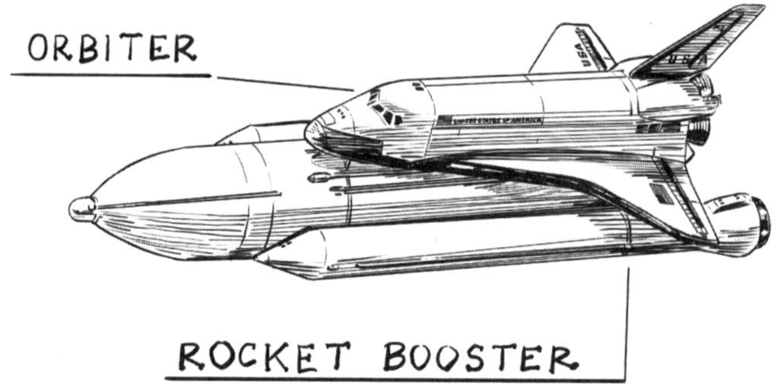

In 1981, *Columbia* was the first space shuttle to launch. NASA would go on to create a whole fleet of shuttles including *Discovery*, *Atlantis*, *Endeavour*, and *Challenger*. Shuttles had a flight deck for the pilots, and places to eat, sleep, and store equipment and supplies. Up to eight people could live on a shuttle, and supplies could last a little over two weeks.

*Columbia*

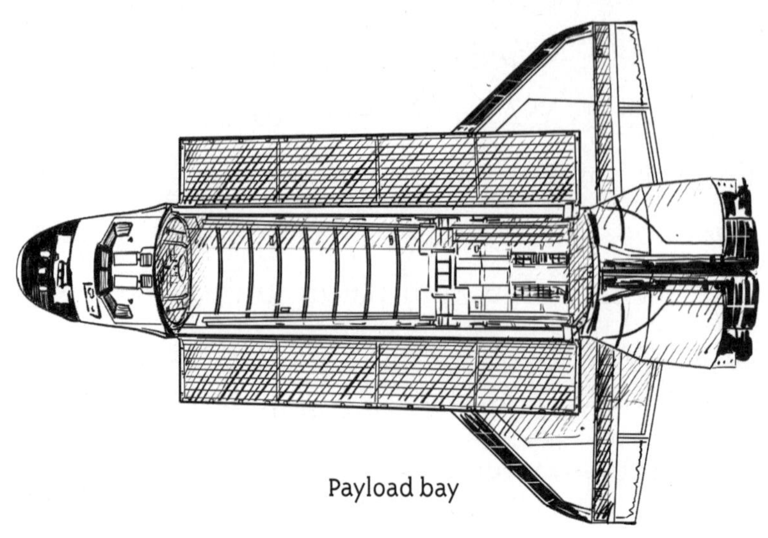


The shuttle also had a payload bay, which takes up the most space on the orbiter. This huge area was used to store satellites that the astronauts were taking into space. A sixty-foot robotic arm would help place these satellites into orbit. Astronauts could also use this space to work on satellites if they needed to be repaired. The payload bay sometimes held Spacelab. Spacelab was a module that was used as a science laboratory where the crew performed experiments and research in a weightless environment.

The United States and the Soviet Union learned a lot as they tried living and working in space. Scientists started asking themselves, *What if?* again. What if several nations worked together? Maybe combining technology and talent could lead to some amazing space achievements and discoveries!

## Weightlessness

Space is a microgravity environment. That means that it seems to have no gravity, and people and objects seem to have no weight. If something is not tied down, it floats when it is inside an orbiting spacecraft. This happens because the spacecraft, and everything in it, is in free fall. Everything is "falling" at the same time.

Imagine you had two balls—one small and light, one big and heavy. If you dropped them at the same time, they would fall at the same rate and hit the ground at the same time, no matter their weight or size. That's because Earth's gravity is pulling them down at the same rate.

Spacecraft are falling toward Earth, too, because gravity is pulling on them. But they are traveling fast enough to stay in orbit. With a little help from thrusters to keep them on course, they never hit the ground. Because the spacecraft is falling, and everything in it is falling, people and objects float and feel weightless.

# CHAPTER 3
# Teamwork

In a speech on January 25, 1984, President Ronald Reagan introduced the idea of an international space station. Like President Kennedy before him, he challenged NASA. "I am directing NASA to develop a permanently manned space station and to do it within a decade," he said.

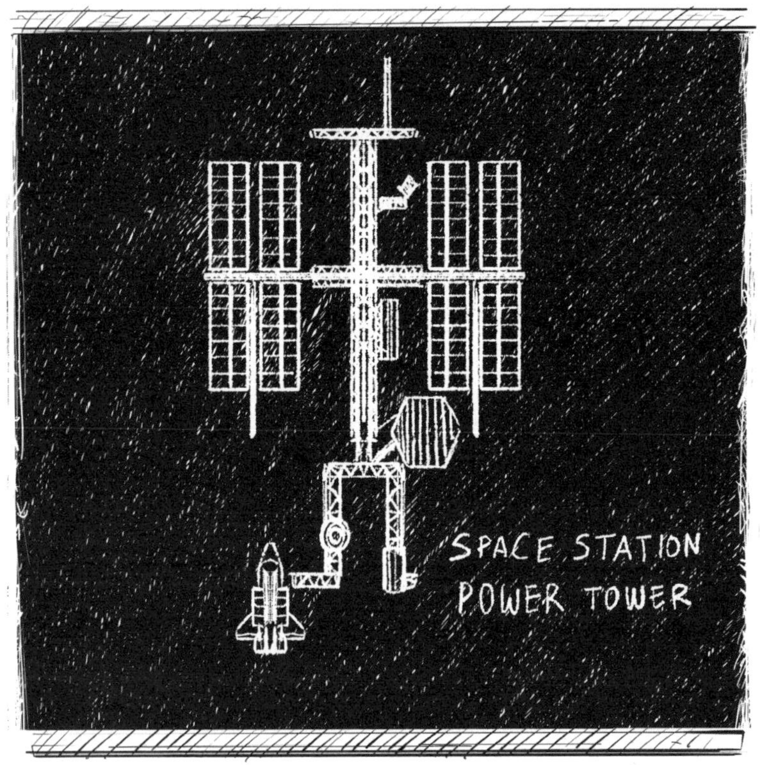


The United States needed partners to complete this goal. Canada, Japan, and many European countries joined in. Over time, they discussed the design and cost. It would take billions of dollars to build something so large in space. They worked on the plan.

Around the same time, the Soviet Union was going through big changes. The large nation had recently broken up into separate countries, and Russia, the largest, was looking for partners in space exploration. So, Russia was invited to join in the building of the International Space Station. NASA and the Russian Space Agency (RSA) signed agreements, along with the Canadian Space Agency (CSA), the Japan Aerospace Exploration Agency (JAXA), and the European Space Agency (ESA). They would combine their knowledge and technology to create the station together.

This wasn't the first time nations had worked together in space. Back in 1975, an Apollo spacecraft from the United States and the Soviet Union's Soyuz 19 spacecraft had a successful docking mission. While these countries had been

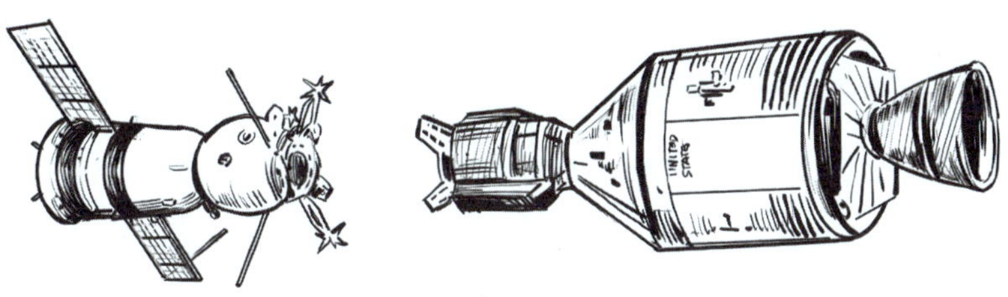

Apollo and Soyuz 19

competing on Earth at the time, they proved that space was a place for cooperation and teamwork.

The first part of the international space station plan was called Shuttle-Mir. It began in 1995 when the American space shuttle *Discovery* docked with the Russian station Mir, which was still in operation. This led to many dockings up through 1998. Crews contained a mix of American and Russian astronauts. These missions were a chance for the two nations to practice living and working

The space shuttle *Atlantis* docking with the Mir space station

together for long periods of time. The Shuttle-Mir missions lasted eight to ten days, with crews of five to ten astronauts per mission.

As the astronauts practiced in space, a team on the ground began building the parts that would eventually be assembled into the ISS. Engineers in

the United States and Russia started constructing modules. The modules would be the rooms of the ISS. Lots of planning was needed because the parts wouldn't be put together until they were in space. So no one knew for sure if they would fit until they got there!

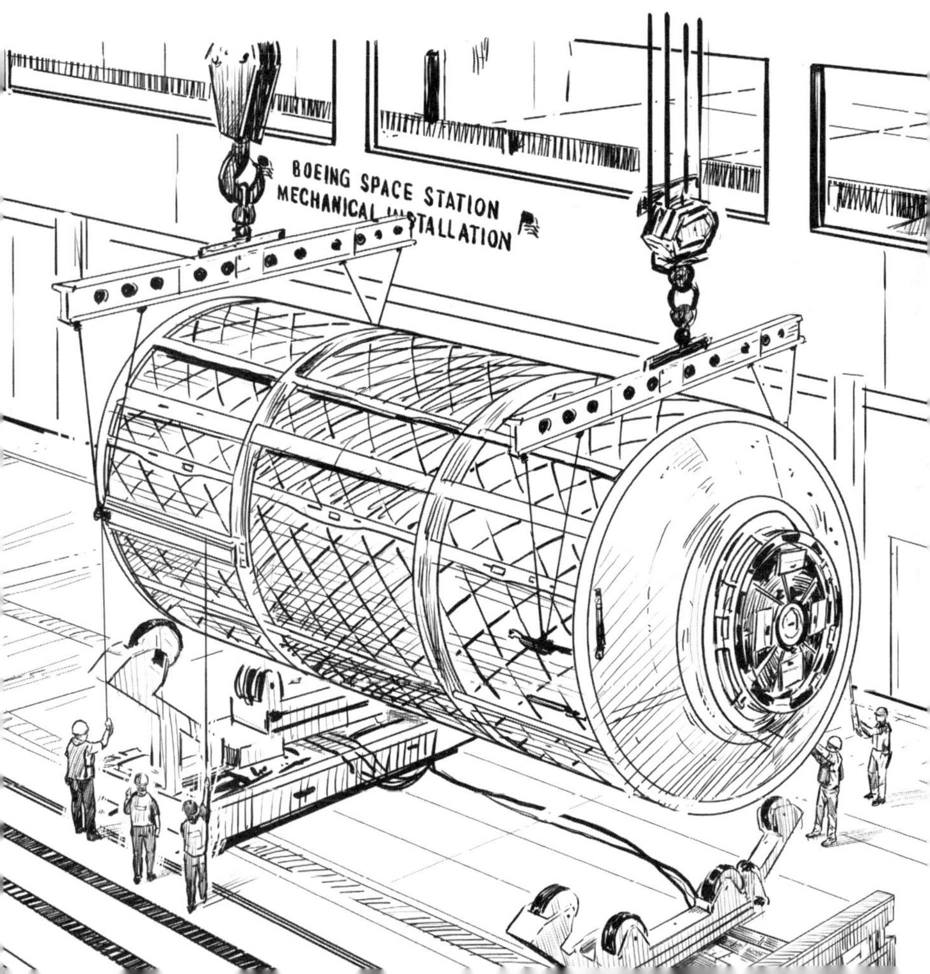

Construction began when the first two modules were assembled 250 miles above Earth. In November 1998, Russia launched a rocket to deliver the module Zarya into orbit. *Zarya* is the Russian word for "sunrise." In early December, the American space shuttle *Endeavour* caught up with Zarya. The shuttle held the module Unity and a crew of both American and Russian astronauts. The shuttle's robotic arm was used to guide Unity and Zarya together. Over the next

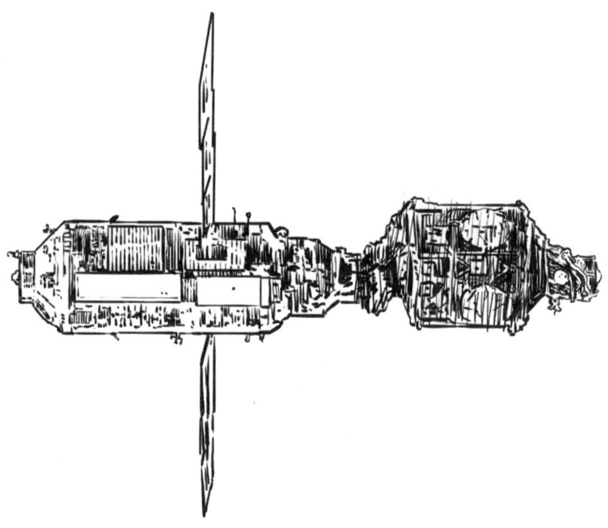

The Zarya (left) and Unity (right) modules attached

Robert D. Cabana and Sergei K. Krikalev

few days, astronauts wearing special suits worked outside the spacecraft connecting power and communication cables between the two modules.

After a few more days, the astronauts could safely enter the new station. They opened the hatches. Robert D. Cabana, an American, and Sergei K. Krikalev, a Russian, entered together. It was a historic moment for both countries and the world. This was the beginning of a huge project that would benefit all humankind.

A crew couldn't actually live in the ISS until 2000, when the Zvezda module was added. William Shepherd from the United States and Sergei Krikalev and Yuri Gidzenko from Russia were the three lucky astronauts who got to be a part of Expedition 1. They lived in the ISS for almost five months until they swapped with another crew. Since that first expedition, there has always been a crew living in the ISS. It hasn't been empty in over twenty years.

William Shepherd and Yuri Gidzenko

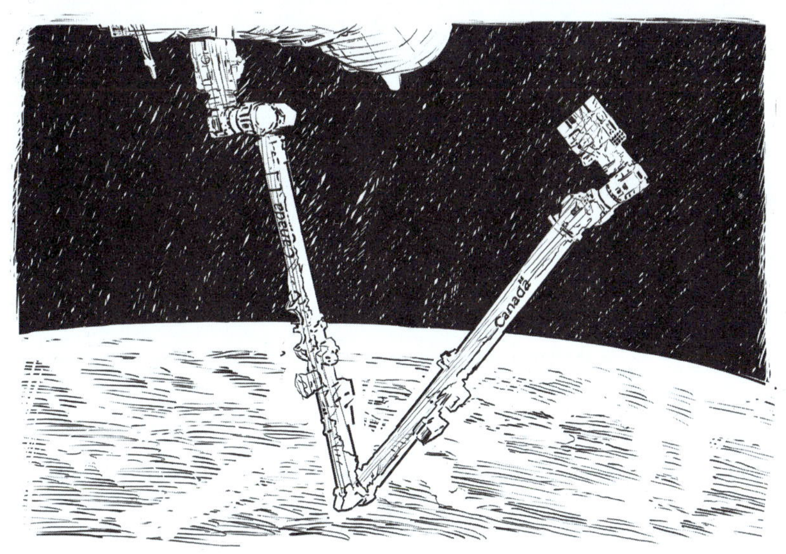


It's hard enough to build a building on Earth. It's even harder to construct something in space. In 2001, a robotic arm designed by the Canadian Space Agency was permanently added to the ISS. This robot made connecting the huge pieces of the station a lot easier than just using a shuttle's robotic arm. The crew controls the almost sixty-foot robotic arm from inside the ISS. It has shoulder, elbow, and wrist joints, just like humans do. Its end is used like a hand to grab onto modules and guide them into place.

Construction continued with parts built by the United States, Russia, Europe, Japan, and Brazil. American and Russian spacecraft brought up these pieces for assembly. Some parts created a framework for the station. Others provided power. Modules held living quarters, laboratories, and control centers. The modules are cylindrical, which means they have rounded sides, similar to cans of soda.

Construction was considered complete in 2011. Since then, nations have continued to add more modules and parts. Commercial companies have also built spacecraft and parts for this largest laboratory in space.

NASA, its partner nations, and companies have had a lot of successes to celebrate throughout the construction. But not all spacecraft missions are successful. Everyone does their best to make sure every detail is perfect. But space travel is dangerous. Sometimes there are accidents.

International Space Station as of March 2011

In 2003, tragedy struck when the space shuttle *Columbia* exploded during reentry into Earth's atmosphere. No shuttles flew for two years until everyone could be sure they were as safe as possible for travel. Scientists and engineers learn when things work, but they also learn when things fail. Every mission has taught them ways to make spacecraft and the space station safer and better for future missions.

The 2003 *Columbia* disaster

The ISS is an amazing achievement in technology. It's an amazing human achievement, too! This project has proven that people from different cultures who live far away from one another on Earth can cooperate and work together in space to learn how to live in a new environment.

## BEAM

Engineers have developed creative ways to construct and transport pieces of the ISS. In 2016, BEAM (the Bigelow Expandable Activity Module), was brought up to the station. This piece was only seven feet wide by seven feet long. The robotic arm attached it to the ISS. Then, over just more than seven hours, astronauts inflated the module to almost double its size with twenty-five short bursts of air.

This construction experiment has shown engineers that station parts might not have to take up as much room on the spacecraft that brings them into orbit. Instead, modules can be inflated or expanded with the help of astronauts once they reach the station.

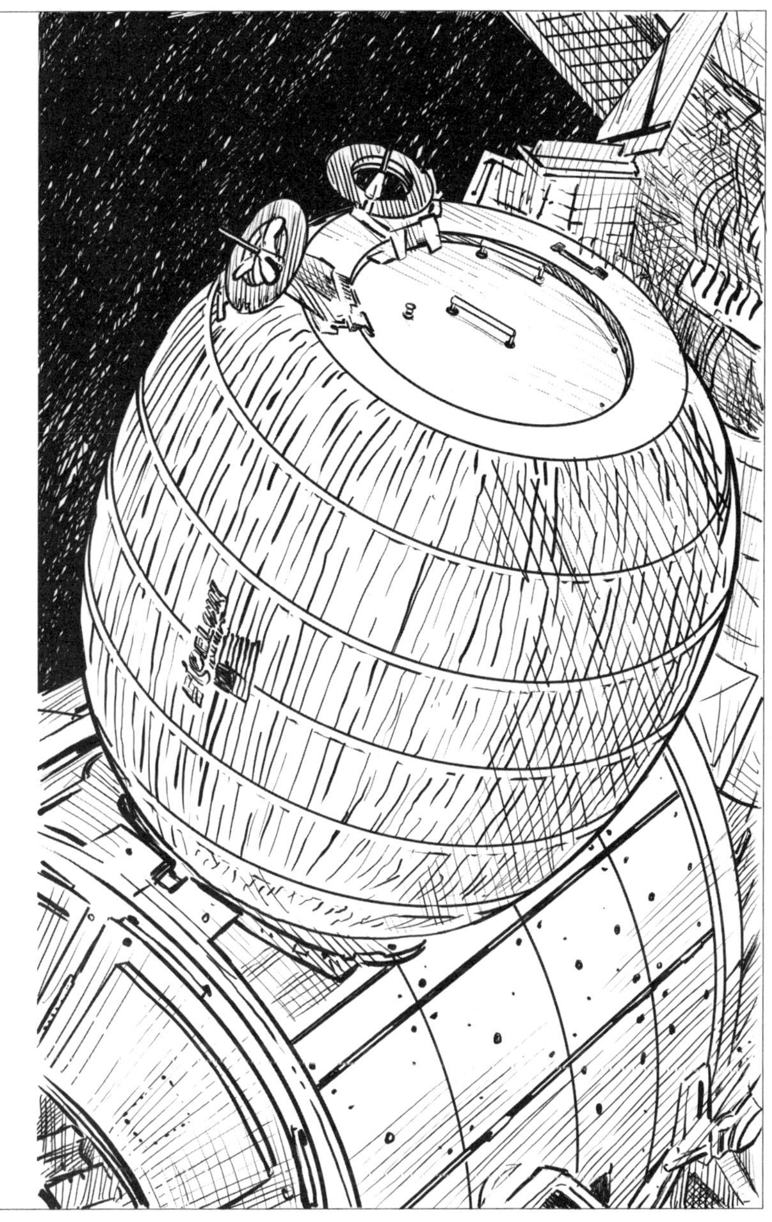

# CHAPTER 4
# A Space Station Tour

People cannot survive in space without special equipment or protection. They wouldn't be able to breathe because there is no oxygen. Their blood and other body fluids would boil because there is no air pressure. The sun's radiation would burn their skin and harm their insides. Temperatures would be extremely hot and extremely cold. So, the engineers worked hard to design the station to be a safe place for the crew to live and work, protecting them from all these dangers of space.

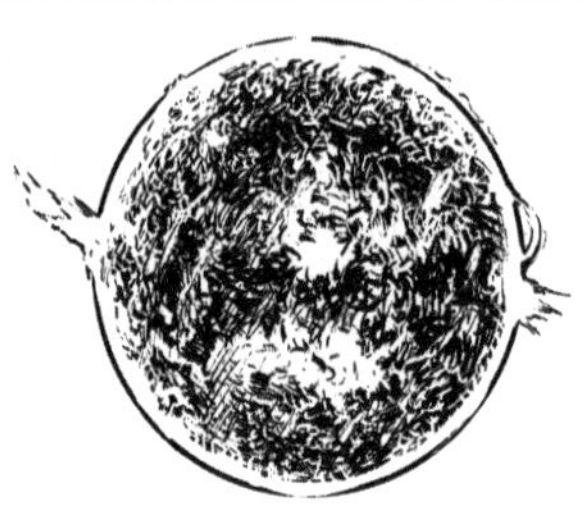

The sun, blazing

Astronaut Daniel W. Bursch with an oxygen generator aboard the ISS

The modules are the rooms of the station. They hold laboratory equipment, living quarters, and power systems. The modules have machines that create air pressure, clean the air of harmful gases, and keep the station at a comfortable temperature. The station can create its own oxygen for astronauts to breathe. The walls and windows of the modules are made of materials that block the sun's harmful rays.

Space junk

The station is made of layers of strong materials to shield astronauts from one of the most harmful dangers of space—space junk. Space junk can be bits of rock. It can also be loose bolts, dropped tools, or pieces that have come off satellites. Because the space station is traveling so fast, even something as tiny as a speck of dust can cause a lot of damage if it collides with the station. The ISS's windows, which are most in danger of being broken, have shutters that close to protect them.

The Russian section of the ISS is at one end of the station. It includes the earliest Zarya and Zvezda modules. Russian astronauts eat, sleep, and do work in these modules. Next comes the US module Unity, which leads to the other modules of the station, called the USOS (United States On-orbit Segment) modules. Astronauts from many different countries live and work in these modules. But the whole crew aboard the ISS often gets together for meals and research, regardless of what country they come from.

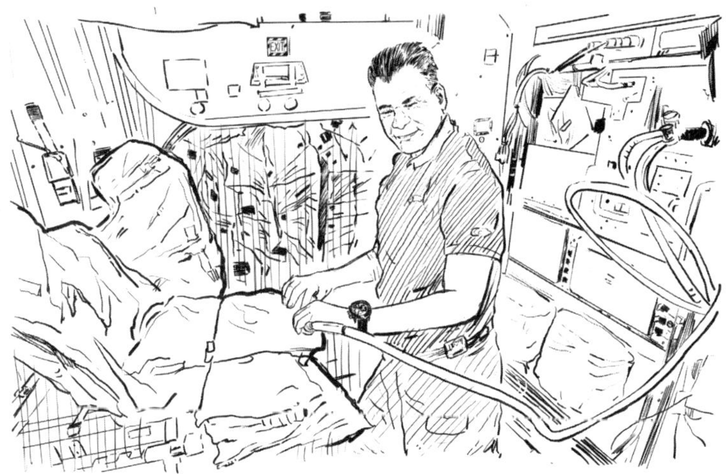


Italian astronaut Paolo Nespoli works inside the Unity module

A space shuttle docked to the ISS

Air locks and docking ports are other necessary parts of the space station. Air locks are the doors in and out of the station for when astronauts need to work outside the ISS. A docking port is like a parking place where a spacecraft from Earth can connect to the station. Eight spaceships can be docked on the ISS at a time. Some spacecraft bring crews to the station. The trip from Earth takes about four hours. Other spacecraft are uncrewed. They bring supplies, experiments, and cargo. Once a spacecraft is docked, the astronauts can open the doors between the spacecraft and the station safely.

The ISS is more than 350 feet long, which is about the length of a football field. The truss is the longest part of the station. This framework of metal beams stretches the length of the ISS. Many of the station's parts are connected to it.

The truss pieces of the ISS

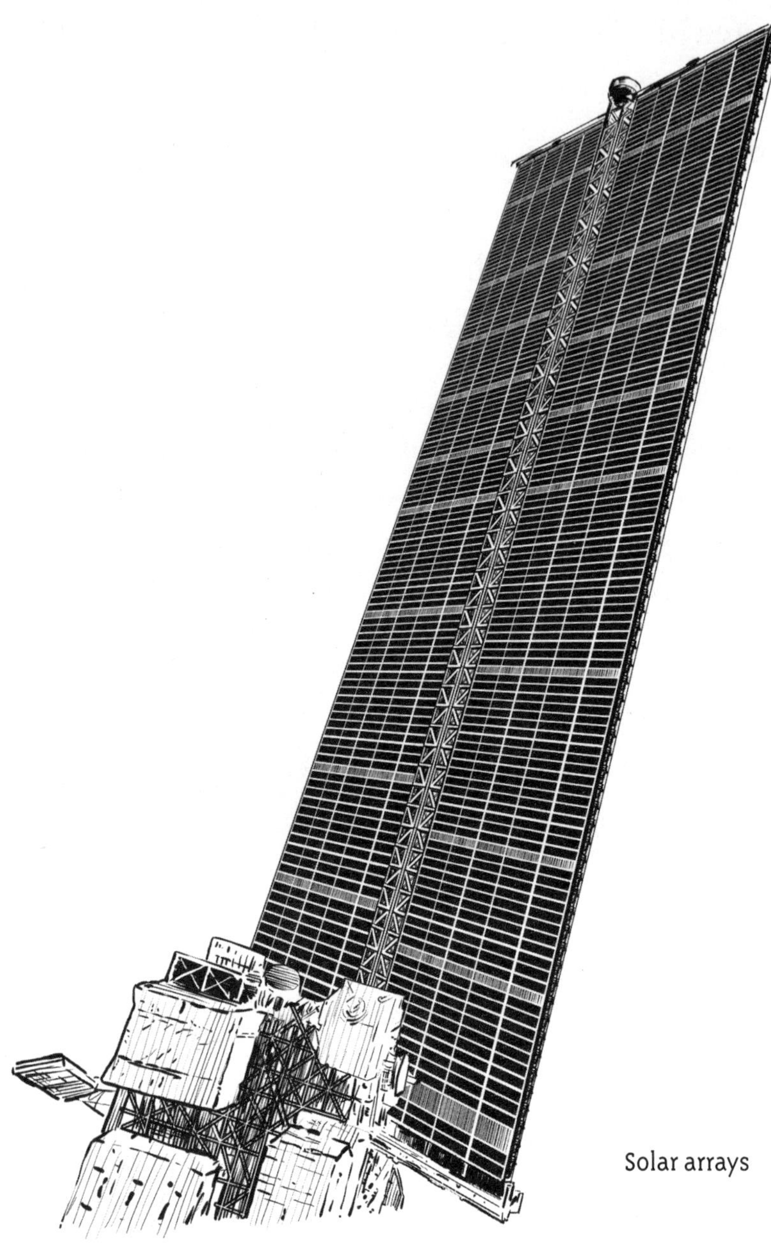
Solar arrays

Solar arrays are mounted on the truss. These large, flat panels are designed to catch the light from the sun and turn it into electricity. This gathered electricity then powers the lights, computers, machinery, and other systems of the ISS. Radiators are also attached to the truss. The radiators are zigzag-shaped panels that help get rid of any extra heat that builds up in the station from the astronauts and their equipment. This keeps the air comfortable enough in the station for the crew to live and work.

The truss also holds storage platforms, spare parts and equipment, and even science experiments. It is a pathway for all the cables and wires that send power and information around the station. It's like a backbone that holds all the parts of the station together.

## What a View!

The ISS has lots of windows, but the cupola has one of the best views! It is attached to the side of the Tranquility module pointing toward Earth. Six windows surround a seventh central window. From here, the crew can watch other astronauts working outside. They can watch for ships arriving and leaving. They can also control the robotic arm from the cupola.

Astronauts observe Earth from these windows. They can see the continents and oceans. They can watch the sunrise and sunset. They can notice how the clouds move. The view is always changing. No wonder it is the favorite spot on the station for many astronauts.

# CHAPTER 5
# Inside and Outside

About seven astronauts live on the ISS at a time. The crews overlap with one another. One crew works together on an expedition. Then, about halfway through, another three or four crew members arrive, and three or four go home to Earth. This new crew is part of a new expedition.

Houston Mission Control Center

The crew spends much of their days doing jobs around the station. They start the day by communicating with mission control to find out their schedule. Mission control is a group of people who manage every mission from a control center on Earth. The main control centers are in the United States and Russia, but there are also smaller control centers in Canada, Japan, and Europe.

## The Christopher C. Kraft, Jr. Mission Control Center

The Mission Control Center at NASA's Johnson Space Center in Houston monitors all human spaceflight. The building never closes. Flight controllers work there twenty-four hours a day. They must be in constant contact with the ISS astronauts.

Flight directors oversee all the flight controllers. The flight controllers have different jobs. Some talk to the astronauts. Others are in charge of the ISS's life-support systems and visiting spacecraft. Flight controllers are also in charge of setting up the astronauts' schedule, tasks they need to do, and goals they need to accomplish.

Inside the ISS, astronauts work in the many modules. The modules are filled with racks. Some are system racks that help run the station. An astronaut's job might be to check or repair the station's many systems. Other astronauts might be working in one of the laboratories. In the labs, racks hold science experiments. The racks on the ISS can hold as many as one hundred experiments at a time. For example, an astronaut might work on an experiment with live bacteria to learn how to keep people from getting sick. Another rack might hold an experiment to watch how ants act in a weightless environment.

If a spacecraft is docked at the station, an astronaut's job might be to unload cargo. This can take months as the crew finds places to store all the new supplies. During times like this, the station can be crowded with zipped-up containers called cargo transfer bags.

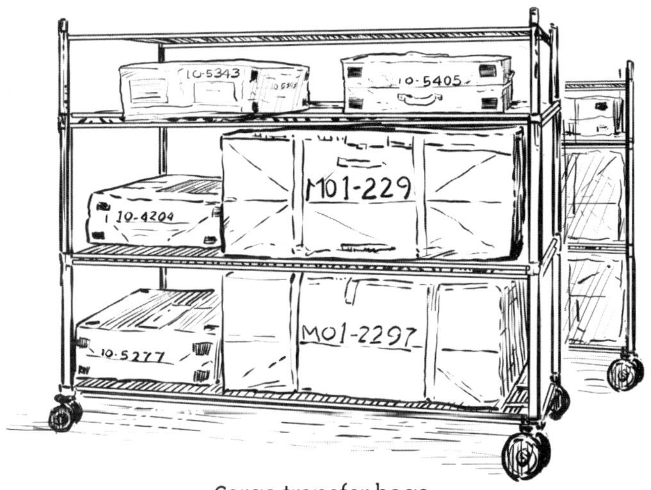


Cargo transfer bags

Since the station is a weightless environment, astronauts don't walk from module to module. They float. Getting around the module while floating is very different from moving from room to room on Earth! Astronauts push off from a surface and keep going in that direction until they push off another surface. Handrails throughout the station help propel them forward, too. They sometimes do flips. When they want to stand still, they tuck their feet under a handrail to stay in place.

Because astronauts float, it doesn't really matter which way is up and which way is down. So almost every surface is used for some purpose. Everywhere they look, there are racks, cabinets, wires, buttons, and dials. There are tools, cameras, and computers. Straps and netting keep storage bags in place on the walls. Surfaces have Velcro, tape, and clips to keep objects in place.

Even though up and down don't matter, crews still think of the part of the station facing Earth as down, and space as up. It's easy to get confused, though, especially if you've been working upside down! So there are signs and room labels throughout the station for direction.

Astronauts can only get to some parts of the station from the outside. If they need to do work on or repair one of these parts, they go on a space walk, or EVA. EVA stands for extravehicular activity. These start at an airlock. That's where the space suits are kept. Astronauts must put on a space suit before they can open the door to go outside.

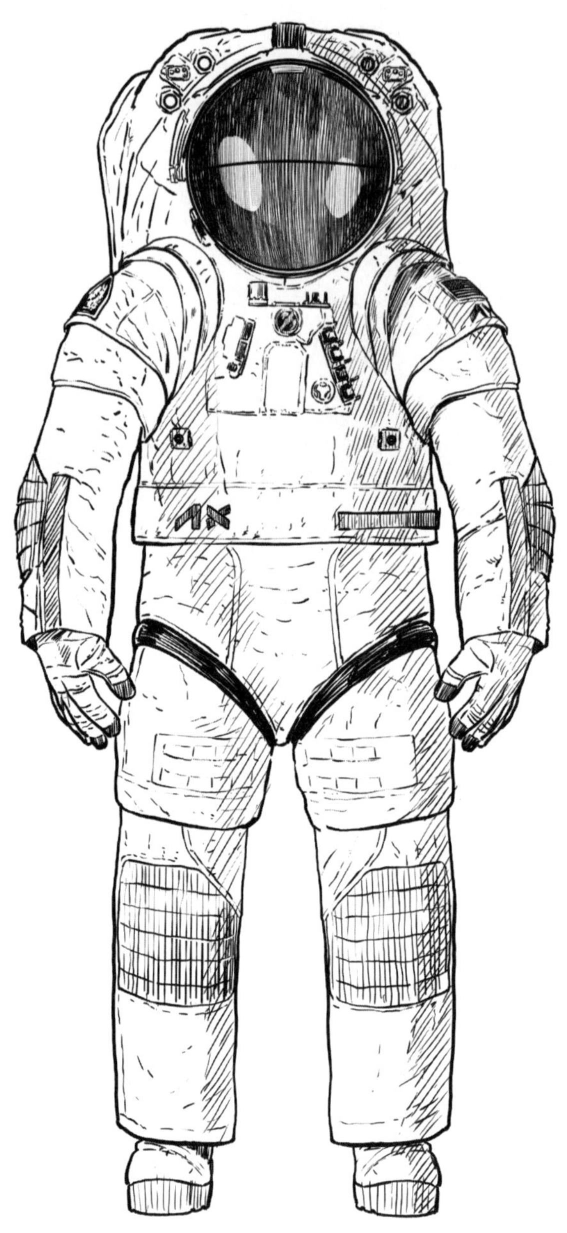

The suits are called EMUs, or Extravehicular Mobility Units. An EMU, like the station itself, has systems to keep the astronaut safe from the dangers of space. The EMU covers their whole body, with gloves for their hands and a helmet for their head. The suit's many layers of special fabrics shield them from the sun's rays and space junk. The suit's white color reflects the sun's light, which helps keep them cool.

The EMU also has air for them to breathe and water for them to drink. Lights and a camera are mounted on the outside. Devices help them talk to the other members of the crew and mission control. Since they often work outside the station for many hours, astronauts have to wear diapers in case they need to go to the bathroom before their work is done.

Spacewalkers are always connected to the station by a tether. If for some reason the tether breaks, they are also wearing a backpack with

thrusters. Short bursts of these thrusters can shoot them back in the direction of the ISS.

Astronauts move along the outside of the station by grasping handholds that are built into the sides of the modules. If they have to travel longer distances to their worksite, they can take a ride on the robotic arm!

## Training for Space

Before astronauts can work in space, they need to practice on Earth! Most training takes place at the Johnson Space Center in Houston, Texas. The astronauts learn about science, swimming, survival, and spacecraft. They practice being weightless. Then they train for their specific mission on the ISS.

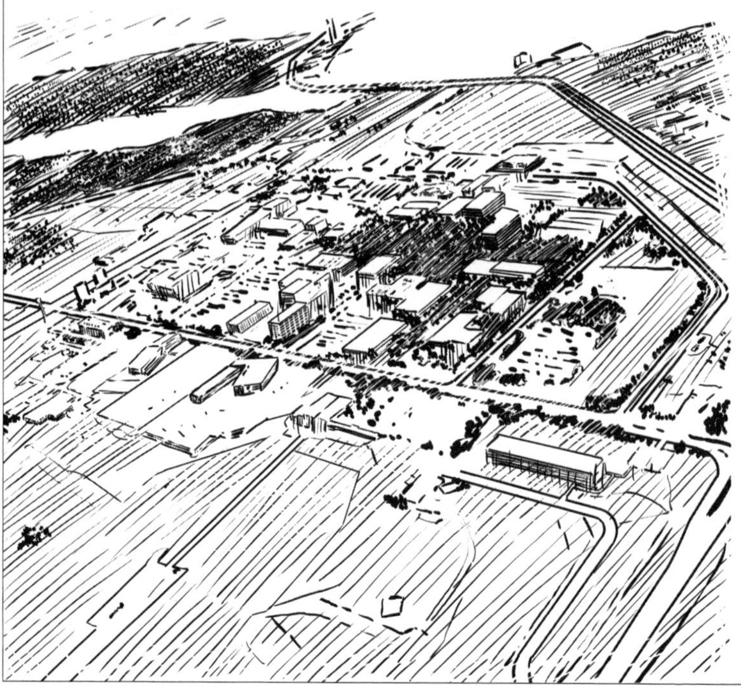

The Johnson Space Center has simulators where astronauts can practice piloting the spacecraft. It also has full-size modules that look just like the ones on the station. Astronauts can work in them to learn what it will be like once they get to space. The center also has one of the world's largest indoor pools. The pool has full-size modules. Astronauts can practice working on the outside of the station underwater. Working underwater feels similar to the weightless experience they will have on a space walk.

All the astronauts have to learn to speak both English and Russian. Some have said this is the hardest part of training!

# CHAPTER 6
# Home Away from Home

For those of us on Earth, the time between one sunrise and the next is twenty-four hours—a full day. The ISS orbits Earth sixteen times in that same amount of time. The crew on the ISS still think of their day as twenty-four hours, even though they see the sun go up and down sixteen times!

Astronauts work hard inside and outside the station. But that is not all they do. The ISS is their home for the months they live up there. So besides taking care of the station, they take care of themselves.

Exercise is important. On Earth, we may run, bike, or play on a playground for exercise. But it's a little different 250 miles above Earth in a weightless environment! Without gravity, bones and muscles can grow very weak. If the astronauts fail to exercise, they won't be able to stand or walk when they arrive back on Earth. So two hours of exercise is a part of everyone's day. The Tranquility module has a treadmill. Astronauts have to strap in to a harness so they don't float off the treadmill's moving floor. Tranquility also has a resistance machine. Using this equipment is like lifting weights. The Destiny lab has an exercise bike that they call the Cycle Ergometer. This bike

doesn't have a seat, wheels, or handlebars. But it does have pedals. Astronauts strap themselves to the machine with a belt and lock their bike shoes into the pedals. When they are not using the bike, it can fold out of the way.

There are several modules in which astronauts can take showers. A shower curtain helps give them privacy. It also keeps water from floating around the station. The shower doesn't spray water from a faucet because it wouldn't work without gravity. Instead, the astronauts shower by using towels filled with soap. They wet the wipes and rub them all over to get clean.

Clothing is stored near the shower. Astronauts wear ordinary clothes, just like at home. But they can't do laundry. So they wear shirts, pants, and underwear many times. When the clothes are too dirty to wear again, they are simply thrown away.

Everybody needs to go to the bathroom, of course. One of the toilets can be found in

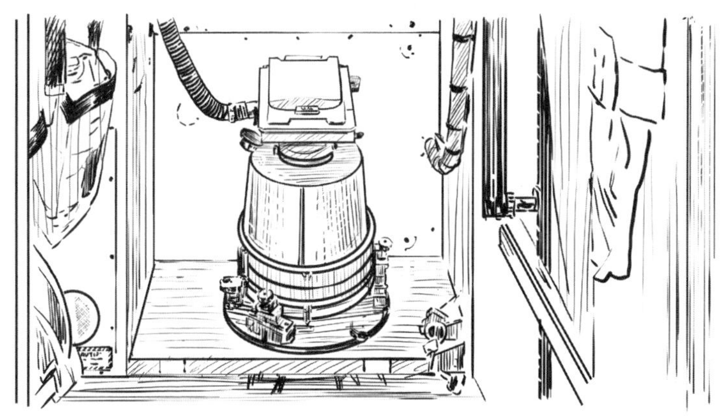

ISS toilet

Tranquility, too. To sit on the toilet, an astronaut straps their feet and body down so they don't float off. Solid waste is sucked into a tank. Urine is sucked into a tube. The station has a Water Recovery System that filters urine so that it can be recycled into drinking and bathing water.

The astronauts also keep healthy by eating healthy. The Unity module is the kitchen and dining room for the USOS side of the space station. Foods have been packaged and labeled on Earth. They are stored in boxes on shelves in the module. The astronauts have many choices—

even peanut butter and jelly. There is a place to warm foods up and keep foods cool. Some foods are ready to eat, while others need to be heated or have water added.

For example, if an astronaut is thirsty, they attach a small pouch of lemonade powder to a water dispenser. Once the pouch is full, they poke a straw in the top and drink, just like a juice pouch on Earth. If the drink wasn't in a pouch with a straw, the lemonade would float right out of their cups!

Some of the most important tools in the kitchen are scissors and spoons. Scissors open packages, and spoons can scoop up every last bit from the bottom of a food pouch. It's impossible to sit together for a meal when everyone is floating. But the station does still have a table. It provides a surface where astronauts can place their food. It's covered with Velcro, tape, and clips to keep everything in place. Even so, eating can sometimes be messy, because bits float away!

The crew creates lots of trash each day. Keeping the station clean is important. But there's not much room to store trash. So, after the crew unloads supplies from an uncrewed spacecraft, they load it back up with trash, like solid waste, kitchen packages, used clothing, and other tools or equipment they don't need anymore. Then the spacecraft is undocked and sent to burn up in Earth's atmosphere.

Astronauts do have some free time. They might call home to talk to family and friends. Others like to watch movies or play games. Some astronauts have even brought up their own musical instruments to play. Free time is also a chance to look out the cupola windows to take in the view and capture pictures of Earth. Astronauts also celebrate and decorate for birthdays and holidays. They even dress up for Halloween!

And even though they have serious work to do, they also know how to have fun! While on Expedition 46, astronaut Scott Kelly's brother Mark sent him a gorilla suit, which was packed along with other supplies in a cargo delivery. Scott saved it until the time was right. Then he dressed in the suit and hid in a storage bag. He jumped out of the bag to surprise the crew and chase them around the station. No one expected a gorilla in space! But everyone had a good laugh.

At the end of the day, it's time for bed. Sleeping quarters are small compartments like closets. The crews strap themselves in their sleeping bags and try to sleep for eight hours a night. The fans, filters, and other equipment on the station are noisy, and the rising and setting of the sun keeps changing the light. Because of this, they often wear earplugs and sleep masks. They need a good night's rest for another busy day!

## Mission Patches

Mission patches have been a part of space programs since the beginning of space exploration. A mission patch is created for every ISS mission. Each time a new group of astronauts works together on the station, they are assigned a mission number and get a new patch. Since the crews overlap and the groups of people change, ISS astronauts usually get two patches during their stay on the station.

The crew works with an artist to design their patch. It typically includes the crew member names and the expedition number. It has images, like spacecraft or country flags, that represent the purpose and people on the mission.

# CHAPTER 7
# Lots to Learn

The ISS is a research laboratory, so it is no surprise that many of its modules are devoted to science. The Russian area of the ISS contains the Nauka laboratory module. In the USOS section, the Harmony module connects three laboratories: Destiny from the United States, Kibo from Japan, and Columbus from Europe. Astronauts perform experiments in these laboratories.

An experiment is when a scientist tests an idea to see if it works as they expect. Scientists perform experiments in laboratories all the time on Earth. But space offers a chance to experiment in a weightless microgravity environment.

Since Earth has gravity, that gravity affects how people and materials act. In space, scientists can do experiments that wouldn't be possible on Earth. They study biology (the study of living things, like people, animals, and plants), agriculture (how things grow), and chemistry (the study of elements that make up all things). They also study physics (the way things move) and many other types of science.

Experiment racks are set up on Earth. Each rack is its own little laboratory for a specific experiment. When the experiment arrives at the station, the astronauts install the rack into one of the laboratories and get to work.

The experiments and observations from the space station have taught us a lot about Earth. The ISS has a unique view from above the atmosphere. It collects data to study weather patterns. It can see storms, fires, and floods, and help warn people before they happen. It can look at the ways Earth has changed over time to help scientists figure out how to best protect it.

ISS research has also taught scientists a lot about space. Equipment on the station collects information about the tiny particles that make up space. Other tools mounted on the outside of the station study spinning stars called pulsars and collapsed stars called black holes. Columbus and Kibo have outdoor platforms so that experiments can be exposed to the harsh conditions of space.

Lots of ISS research focuses on the human body. Cells, the tiny building blocks that make up all people, are easier to grow in space. Microscopes on the ISS help make it possible to see these cells. Astronauts have done many cell experiments to test medicines that could help cure diseases.

Destiny and Kibo have glove boxes. The Microgravity Science Glovebox is a sealed space. Its sides are clear to see inside. Gloves are attached to holes on the sides. The astronauts can safely

work on an experiment that might be dangerous inside this box. For example, they have studied flames and how they burn in microgravity inside the glove boxes.

Many of the experiments have helped scientists as they plan for more space exploration. Trips beyond Earth's orbit could take many years. Crews would not be able to come home between missions. The spacecraft would be too far away to dock with a supply delivery. So some of the experiments have prepared the station to be more self-sufficient. That means it would be able to supply the ship and its crew with everything they would need. The station can already recycle water and create oxygen. But ISS researchers have experimented with even more ways to be self-sufficient.

The ISS's Vegetable Production System, nicknamed Veggie, grows fresh food without having to use too much power or water. If astronauts needed to go on a longer trip, they could grow their own food instead of having to bring it all along.

Vegetable Production System

3D printers on the space station have also been helpful. They can print plastic and metal pieces. These printers could be used to make replacement parts for equipment if something should break on a longer trip.

Astronauts also get help from robots inside the ISS. A ball-shaped camera roams around the station taking pictures and filming the crew to document what they are doing. Other robots called Astrobees can sense changes in sound to help warn astronauts in case of trouble. Astrobees also practice moving through the station, by tossing themselves, hopping around, or grasping smooth surfaces. Just like the crew, robots are practicing for future missions.

Astrobees

## Twin Astronauts

Scott and Mark Kelly are twin brothers who were important subjects in one of the ISS's experiments called the Twins Study.

Scott and Mark Kelly

As identical twins, Scott and Mark have the same genes. Scott Kelly spent a year in space from March 2015 to March 2016. Mark Kelly stayed on Earth. When Scott came back after his mission, scientists were able to study how his body had changed compared to Mark's.

Six months after returning to Earth, the only changes to Scott's body that had remained were changes to the tiny parts inside his body's cells. But overall, Scott was healthy. This important experiment showed scientists that human bodies continue to work well even after long stays in space. This will help as astronauts take longer trips outside of Earth's orbit.

# CHAPTER 8
# Future Missions

The ISS is 250 miles above Earth, and it's traveling five miles per second. Even though it is so far away and is moving so fast, you might be able to spot it in the night sky. At certain times, in certain places, the space station looks like a bright, fast-moving airplane. It appears a few hours before sunrise or a few hours after sunset. It's not giving off its own light. The sun's light is reflecting, or bouncing, off its surface.

The ISS has been orbiting Earth for more than twenty years. It's quite amazing to think that humans figured out how to live and work in the harsh environment of space. It took a lot of science and imagination. It took teamwork. Thousands of people in different countries designed and

built the parts. Engineers found ways to get those parts into space. Crews worked together to keep the station going every day.

But the ISS can't keep orbiting Earth forever. It is a piece of equipment. And like all equipment, it will wear out. The worn-out parts could make living in the ISS unsafe. These parts would need to be fixed or replaced. That would cost a lot of time and money. Scientists at the space agencies have decided that it will soon be time to put the time and money toward different projects, like exploring the moon and Mars.

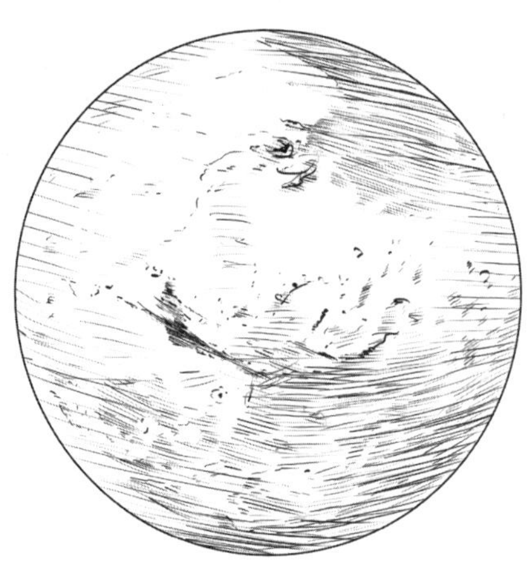

Mars

The ISS will operate through 2030. The space agencies thought a lot about what to do with the ISS after that. They considered taking it apart piece by piece so that parts could be used again or brought back down to Earth to show in museums. But it took many years to put the station together, and it would take many years to take it apart. Plus, NASA no longer has a space shuttle fleet to bring the large pieces back.

They thought about parking the ISS in a higher orbit, without a crew. However, spacecraft do not yet exist that could travel into such a high orbit. And the station would eventually break down, and no one would be on board to fix it. It would fall to Earth someday, and they couldn't control where the pieces might fall. That could be dangerous for people and other living things on Earth.

Instead, the space agencies have decided to deorbit the ISS in a controlled way. Deorbit means to take it out of orbit. The crew will leave. Without a crew to keep it on course, the station will orbit lower and lower. It will get a final push out of orbit by a spacecraft. Then it will fall

through Earth's atmosphere. Most of its parts will burn up. Some of the larger pieces, like the truss parts, will fall safely into the ocean, away from people.

Throughout the history of space exploration, each new experience has better prepared explorers for the next one. We have learned so much from the ISS. All of that research and discovery has prepared people for longer space trips to the moon and Mars in the future. That was one of the goals of the ISS.

But the ISS had another goal, too—to get kids excited about math, science, engineering, and technology. Through various programs, students have communicated with the ISS astronauts, worked with them on experiments from Earth, and even designed experiments that went into orbit. The International Space Station has inspired many kids all over the world to think about going into space. A kid like you might one day be a crew member on a future mission beyond Earth's orbit!

AL SPACE STATION

## Space Characters

Some very famous characters have been able to experience the weightlessness of space in the ISS. Astronauts have brought up Barbie, Buzz Lightyear, Baby Yoda, an Angry Bird, and Smokey Bear toys. But Snoopy, from the comic strip *Peanuts*, has been in space more than any other character.

In 1968, NASA asked Charles Schulz, Snoopy's creator, if Snoopy could be a mascot for the Space Flight Awareness Program. Silver Snoopy awards, pins with the image of Snoopy dressed in a space suit, became a way to recognize people who contribute to the safety and improvement of spaceflight.

Snoopy made his first trip into space on the Apollo 8 mission in 1968, as astronauts Frank Borman, Jim Lovell, and Bill Anders wore Silver Snoopy pins. Spacecraft have been named after

Snoopy. So have the communications caps that astronauts wear. In 2019, astronauts Jessica Meir, Christina Koch, and Snoopy sent a Thanksgiving greeting to Earth. A stuffed Snoopy toy floated along with the astronauts on the ISS at the same time as a Snoopy balloon, dressed as an astronaut, floated above the streets of New York City in the Macy's Thanksgiving Day Parade. Snoopy even took a ride in the space capsule on the Artemis mission to the moon in 2022.

## Timeline of the International Space Station

| | |
|---|---|
| 1957 | The Soviet Union sends Sputnik 1 into orbit |
| 1971 | The Soviet Union launches Salyut 1, the first space station |
| 1973 | NASA launches its first space station, named Skylab |
| 1984 | United States president Ronald Reagan directs NASA to develop an international space station within ten years |
| 1986 | The Soviet Union launches the first module of the Mir space station |
| 1995–1998 | Astronauts practice docking, living, and working together during Shuttle-Mir missions |
| 1998 | Construction of the ISS begins with modules Zarya and Unity |
| 2000 | The first ISS crew lives on the ISS during Expedition 1 |
| 2001 | The US Destiny laboratory is added to the station |
| 2008 | The European Space Agency's Columbus and Japan's Kibo laboratories are added to the ISS |
| 2011 | The Space Shuttle program ends with *Atlantis* after 135 missions |
| 2012 | The first commercial spacecraft, SpaceX's *Dragon*, is used to bring supplies to the ISS |
| 2021 | Russia's Nauka laboratory is added to the Zvezda module |
| 2023 | A three-year project focused on installing new solar arrays on the ISS is completed |
| 2031 | NASA plans to start deorbiting the ISS |

# Timeline of the World

**bya = billion years ago**

| | |
|---|---|
| 13.8 bya | The universe begins to grow from a small hot point in space |
| 3.7 bya | Life first appears on Earth |
| c. 300,000 years ago | First humans appear on Earth |
| c. 3,000 BCE | People start writing down history |
| 150 CE | Egyptian astronomer Ptolemy suggests an Earth-centered universe |
| 1543 | Polish astronomer Nicolaus Copernicus suggests a sun-centered solar system |
| 1609 | Italian astronomer Galileo Galilei uses a telescope to observe the moon |
| 1687 | British scientist Sir Isaac Newton develops his law of gravity |
| 1926 | American scientist Robert Goddard launches the first successful liquid-fueled rocket |
| 1969 | US astronauts Neil Armstrong and Buzz Aldrin are the first people to walk on the moon's surface |
| 1990 | The space shuttle *Discovery* delivers the Hubble Space Telescope into Earth's orbit to take pictures of outer space |
| 2021 | NASA lands a robotic rover, called *Perseverance*, on the surface of the planet Mars |
| 2022 | Missions begin in the Artemis program for more exploration on the moon and future trips to Mars |

# Bibliography


***Books for young readers**

*Holden, Henry M. ***The Coolest Job in the Universe: Working Aboard the International Space Station***. Berkeley Heights, NJ: Enslow Publishers, 2013.

Howell, Elizabeth. "International Space Station: Everything You Need to Know about the Orbital Laboratory." Space.com. Updated February 23, 2024. https://www.space.com/16748-international-space-station.html.

"International Space Station." NASA. Updated January 30, 2025. https://www.nasa.gov/international-space-station/.

Leary, Warren E. "For the First Time, Astronauts Enter International Space Station." ***New York Times***. December 11, 1998. https://www.nytimes.com/1998/12/11/us/for-the-first-time-astronauts-enter-international-space-station.html.

"Nancy Currie-Gregg, #Astronaut (Texas A&M) Public Lecture PM 04.06.2019." July 13, 2022. YouTube video, 58:47. https://www.youtube.com/watch?v=CJv698MZ2sM&t=282s.

NASA Johnson. ***International Space Station***. Updated April 11, 2025. YouTube playlist. https://www.youtube.com/playlist?list=PLTXQuaxXBKKwtqw9fmVw9YnMKxz6FcmWf.

*Rector, Rebecca Kraft. ***The International Space Station***. New York: Children's Press, 2022.

*Stott, Carole. ***Space Exploration***. New York: DK Publishing, 2014.

"Web Extra: International Space Station Tour." April 22, 2021. YouTube video, 29:35. https://www.youtube.com/watch?v=AErpXJq67LM.

*Williams, Dave, and Loredana Cunti. ***To Burp or Not to Burp: a Guide to Your Body in Space***. Toronto: Annick Press, 2016.

**Websites**

www.airandspace.si.edu (Smithsonian National Air and Space Museum)

www.asc-csa.gc.ca/eng/ (Canadian Space Agency)

www.esa.int (European Space Agency)

www.issnationallab.org (ISS National Laboratory)

www.humans-in-space.jaxa.jp/en/ (Japan Aerospace Exploration Agency)

www.nasahunch.com (NASA HUNCH mission)

WHOHQ®